Original title:
Life, Explained Through Coffee

Copyright © 2025 Creative Arts Management OÜ
All rights reserved.

Author: Mariana Leclair
ISBN HARDBACK: 978-1-80566-034-7
ISBN PAPERBACK: 978-1-80566-329-4

Percolating Dreams

Mornings brew with hopes so bright,
Java jive to start the fight.
Sips of wisdom, dark and bold,
In the cup, our dreams unfold.

Stirring thoughts like sugar sweet,
Frothy lattes, can't be beat.
Espressos pack a punch, oh yes!
In each sip, we find success.

A Cupful of Moments

Caffeine highs and sugar lows,
In each cup, a story grows.
Mugs of joy and spills of cheer,
Every drop, a memory near.

Stale brews like past mistakes,
New blends, oh, the joy they make!
Sip by sip, we dance and spin,
In our cups, let chaos win.

Grounds for Reflection

Coffee grounds, like thoughts, steeped deep,
In the mugs, we laugh and weep.
Filters catching what we hide,
In the brew, our fears reside.

Pouring out the bitter parts,
Crafting art with rusted carts.
With each cup, perspective shifts,
In our hands, the world uplifts.

The Aroma of Tomorrow

Scented whispers of what's to come,
Frothy dreams in a distant hum.
Cups raised high, we toast to fate,
To the grind and its playful state.

A drizzle of syrup for that thrill,
Each spill a moment, catch the chill.
Tomorrow waits in every brew,
With every sip, we start anew.

The Art of Infusion

In the morning light, I brew my cheer,
A splash of madness, with coffee near.
Sipping joy, it dances on my tongue,
A brewed-up tale, forever young.

Beans of wonder, they twist and swirl,
Hot water flows, the pot starts to whirl.
Each sip's a story, a giggle or sigh,
With frothy dreams, I'll surely fly.

Add a dash of sugar, a sprinkle of glee,
The secret potion that sets me free.
Stirring thoughts like a spoon in a cup,
Awake and laughing, I sip it up.

So here's to the brew, both bold and bright,
Frothy whispers keep my spirits light.
With every slurp, a chuckle is found,
In this caffeinated world, joy abounds.

Dark Notes and Light Brews

In shadowy mugs, the tales unfold,
Dark roast secrets, as stories are told.
Espresso shots like little bursts of cheer,
Caffeine confessions, nothing to fear.

Creamy froth with a dash of delight,
Blending all worries from morning to night.
Lattes swirl like a dance on the floor,
Sips of laughter, who could ask for more?

When the beans are ground, listen to the fun,
Each gurgle a giggle, the day's begun.
From bitter to sweet, flavors unite,
In each cup poured, a small pure delight.

At the bottom of cups, wisdom awaits,
Funny reflections on charred, cracked plates.
So toast with your brew, and chuckle anew,
In the world of coffee, laughter is true.

Caramelized Aspirations

In the pot, hopes brew and swirl,
Beans dance like dreams in a twirl.
Stirring in sugar, a dash of cream,
Sweet thoughts rise, like a coffee dream.

Sipping slowly, I laugh out loud,
At plans that never leave the crowd.
We spill the beans on our wild schemes,
Caramel drips from our craziest dreams.

Shots of Clarity

One shot in, and my brain's awake,
Thoughts perk up, like a first date flake.
Second shot, and the giggles bloom,
As caffeine chases away the gloom.

With a frothy sip, I see so clear,
Like magic fairies just appeared here.
Darling espresso, you're my wise friend,
Sharing secrets, 'til the very end.

Milky Ways and Mocha Dreams

Creamy galaxies swirl in my cup,
Chocolate flavors just bubble up.
In this cosmos of froth and whip,
I savor each starry little sip.

Mocha waves crash on shores of cheer,
Changing tides of joy draw near.
I laugh with the beans, so sly, so spry,
As galaxies dance in this café sky.

The Ritual of Reflection

Morning brew, a ritual so fine,
In the steam, thoughts twist and entwine.
Pour the potion, watch it steep,
A sip of solace, my secrets keep.

A cuppa joy, with a side of glee,
Pondering life under this old tree.
With each sip, I chuckle and muse,
Reflecting on choices, the morning's excuse.

Infused Insights

A cup of warmth, it starts the day,
Beans jump in, and dance away.
Splash of cream, a wink of glee,
Sip by sip, just let it be.

Stirrers swirl, like life's great mess,
Sugar cubes, a sweet finesse.
A jolt of joy, a buzz of cheer,
Where's my coffee? It's nowhere near!

Mugs may spill, grounds may fly,
Like random thoughts that drift on by.
But every drop's a story told,
As dreams arise, bold and gold.

A Medley of Melodies

Espresso shots, a quickened beat,
They sing of mornings, oh so sweet.
Pour it strong, let laughter flow,
   Sips of joy in every row.

Mochas blend with hints of spice,
   Every joke warms up the slice.
A cappuccino's frothy crown,
Makes the frowns just tumble down.

With each refill, the fun expands,
Friends gather close, with coffee in hand.
A melody of sips and smiles,
   Bursting joy for endless miles.

Roasted Revelations

Beans go crackle, stories reign,
Rich aroma, a gentle gain.
Brewed adventures, steaming hot,
What wisdom lies in every pot?

Sips of caffeine, laugh lines grow,
A splash of chaos, a roasted show.
Life's ups and downs in every brew,
Who knew a latte could see me through?

Drips of humor, spills of cheer,
Each taste reveals what we hold dear.
So hold that mug, and let it shine,
A potion brewed, both yours and mine.

The Alchemy of Beans

Pour a cup, let's mix and play,
Brewed emotions, day by day.
A dash of fun, a pinch of strain,
In coffee's magic, we find our gain.

You heat it up, then watch it brew,
Life's surprises come into view.
Caffeine chuckles, laughter abounds,
Transforming us, in tight-knit rounds.

Stirring dreams in every blend,
Who knew beans could be a friend?
So drink it up, each playful sip,
A comedy in every trip.

Moments in a Mug

Every morning has its dose,
A jolt to shake off sleepy prose.
Steam rising, a perfect view,
A bitter start, yet oh so true.

Sips of laughter, spills of fate,
Caffeine dreams that just can't wait.
A dance of milk, a splash of fun,
Together we brew, the day's begun.

Connected by Coffee

Two cups clink, a toast of cheer,
With every sip, the world feels clear.
Friends unite, through froth and foam,
In this café, we find our home.

Banters flow like steaming brews,
Jokes percolate, we trade our views.
A shot of espresso for every laugh,
In caffeine's grip, we find our path.

Blends of Destiny

In the grinder, fate does swirl,
Beans collide, as flavors twirl.
A pinch of sugar, a dash of spice,
In every cup, a twist of nice.

Some like it black, some love the cream,
Each brew, a quirky little dream.
From mocha mischief to latte lore,
We sip sweet secrets we can't ignore.

Savoring Silence

In the quiet, a mug resides,
Warmth within, no need to hide.
Sips of solace, a gentle pause,
In each gulp, we find our cause.

The world outside can rush and race,
But here, we linger, just embrace.
With every drop, our worries cease,
A calm connection, brewed in peace.

Pouring Over Paradoxes

It's bitter in the morning, sweet by noon,
A cup of chaos, served with a spoon.
Stirred by dreams, brewed in strife,
Each sip's a riddle, much like life.

Hot or cold, we dance on a whim,
With caffeine courage, our chances slim.
We brew our worries, froth our fears,
Raise mugs to the madness, toast with cheers!

Espresso of Experience

A shot of boldness, quick and bright,
Chasing shadows, embracing light.
With every pour, a tale unfolds,
Sweeten it slowly, watch it mold.

Lattes swirl with tales untold,
Spicy secrets, creamy and bold.
Sip it slow, let flavors linger,
Each cup reveals a different finger.

Whispers in the Froth

In the foam, secrets softly hide,
Like on a journey, we take a ride.
Marshmallow clouds, giggles in steam,
Sipping comfort, chasing a dream.

Bubbles pop with each little joke,
As espresso laughs, it's never broke.
Pouring thoughts like sugar in,
Stirring joy where we begin.

Stirring the Soul

A swirl of joy, a hint of spice,
Dancing flavors, oh so nice.
With every stir, a little zing,
Awakening the heart to sing.

Caramel laughs and mocha sighs,
Mirthful moments, a sweet surprise.
Pour another round, let good times flow,
In this café of life, we steal the show!

Brewed Bonds

In a cup we share our tales,
Stirring joy, amid the gales.
Sugar sweetens our delight,
Friends together, mornings bright.

From the pot, we pour our dreams,
In steamy swirls, life seems.
Laughter bubbles, froth takes flight,
Caffeine giggles, pure and light.

A Sip of Solace

When the world's a bitter grind,
A warm mug soothes the mind.
Sipping slow, we find the cheer,
A dash of cream wipes out the fear.

With every gulp, worries flee,
Java hugs, a remedy.
Chasing blues with roasty flair,
Witty brews, beyond compare.

Grounds for Growth

From the grounds, new dreams arise,
Like dandelions reaching skies.
Brewing bold, we take a stand,
Embracing mess, it's truly grand.

Filters catch our quirks and strife,
Brewed together, oh, that life!
With each sip, we learn to thrive,
In this cup, we come alive.

Latte Lessons

Foamy shapes, a playful art,
Every sip, it warms the heart.
Perfect rosettas, life's small tricks,
Espresso shots, sweet caffeine kicks.

Swirling cream, like dreams we chase,
A pinch of joy, a swirling grace.
Every mug tells tales of old,
With every drink, new stories unfold.

The Cup That Holds Us

In the morning sun, we brew,
A little chaos, a sip or two.
Spilled beans here, laughter there,
A mug of joy, without a care.

Espresso shots like dreams at dawn,
Frothy giggles keep us drawn.
Caffeine buzz, we dance around,
In this cup, our joy is found.

Bitter Brews and Sweet Sips

Bitter grounds that spill on floors,
Like the chaos behind locked doors.
Sweet sugar kisses, a warming hug,
Stirring troubles like a playful mug.

Sipping slowly, we chat and tease,
Over steamy brews, it's all a breeze.
Life's a mix of dark and light,
In every cup, we find delight.

Blend of the Present

Pour the beans, the day's elixir,
Laughs blend in, life feels quicker.
Each whiff a tale, each sip a jest,
A rollercoaster, that's the quest.

Milk froth swirls like stories spun,
In a cup of warmth, we find our fun.
Chasing spills like playful dreams,
In coffee chat, nothing's as it seems.

Hot and Cold: A Pour

Hot mugs clash with ice-cold cups,
Like mischief with a side of ups.
Sipping slow, we trade a grin,
In this brew, where jokes begin.

Steam rises like the day's odd quirks,
With every gulp, the laughter lurks.
Blend it all, sweet or bold,
In every sip, a laugh unfolds.

Steaming Conversations

Steam rising high, like dreams we chase,
In cups of warmth, we find our place.
Spilled secrets shared in sips and grins,
With each round brewed, the laughter begins.

Caffeine chats can lighten the load,
A dash of sugar on every road.
Life's mysteries swirl like frothy cream,
Let's toast to chaos and every scheme.

Bittersweet Reminiscence

Oh, the days of youth, they brewed so bold,
But all good things, they must grow old.
Espresso shots of dreams once bright,
Fade into shadows under dim light.

Each sip recalls those moments lush,
With mocha memories, we feel the rush.
Bittersweet notes in every blend,
We sip, we laugh, and sometimes mend.

Latte Lamentations

Frothy fables swirl in every cup,
As life spills over, we mix it up.
Creamy wishes dissolve like steam,
In melty mugs, we find our dream.

Spilling beans with every pour,
A latte art that keeps us to the core.
With every gulp, a tale we weave,
In froth we trust, in blend we believe.

Drips of Destiny

One drip at a time, we brew our fate,
A coffee clock that won't wait.
The filter catches all our fears,
While mugs collect our hopes and cheers.

As beans collide, we laugh and muse,
Decaf dilemmas or bold life's ruse?
With every drop, our plans might shift,
But in this cup, we find our gift.

Awakening Brew

Morning routine, so caffeinated,
My cup's a friend, never outdated.
In every sip, a jolt of glee,
Awake, alert, oh joy to be!

Spilt some grounds, watch them dance,
My kitchen's chaos gives me a chance.
A splash of cream, a sugar rush,
Who knew a mug could cause such a fuss?

Brew it dark, or make it light,
In every cup, a comic plight.
Drink it slow, then gulp it fast,
Caffeine dreams, oh please, just last!

At work we sip, the gossip flows,
With every cup, the banter grows.
A shot of brew, and jokes ignite,
Life's absurd, but coffee's right!

Java Journeys

Take a stroll, but don't forget,
Your coffee cup is your best bet.
Adventure's near with each warm sip,
Just don't spill it on this trip!

Cloudy skies or sunny cheer,
With java close, there's naught to fear.
At every drain, a splash, a smile,
Coffee's magic lasts awhile!

From beans to brew, a funny chase,
The barista grins, it's quite the race!
Add some spice, a dash of fun,
In every cup, the world's well spun!

Sit on benches, share a laugh,
Order one—don't do the math!
A java journey, what a ride,
Fueled by brewed delight inside!

The Espresso of Existence

Is life a shot, so bold, so neat?
Or a slow brew, a comfy seat?
Each tiny sip, a thought to share,
The frothy mustache bows to flair!

In the café, we ponder deep,
Caffeine-laden dreams we keep.
With every cup, the truths we find,
A sip of wisdom, one of kind!

An espresso shot, quick and bright,
Wakes the senses, sparks the light.
Though jittery laughs may come about,
With coffee in hand, we scream and shout!

At the bottom, what's left to see?
The dregs of life, so bitterly.
But top it off, and start anew,
With java dreams, we chase what's true!

Sips of Solitude

In a quiet nook, I take my time,
A steaming cup, a simple rhyme.
With every sip, the world slips away,
Lost in thoughts, I merrily stray.

Alone, but oh, so not lonely,
With coffee's warmth, I'm never phony.
Each drip and drop, a gentle hum,
Solitude sings, I've just begun!

Sugar swirls and cream's embrace,
I sip and think, my private space.
Every sip, a chuckle or grin,
Where quiet moments always win!

But watch out for that daring breeze,
A rogue cup's spill, oh what a tease!
In hidden sips, my thoughts collide,
With coffee close, I take the ride!

The Brewed Sunset

In a cup of warmth, the day begins,
With frothy dreams and coffee spins.
Each sip a giggle, a playful tease,
Like waking up to a friendly breeze.

Espresso shots like rocket fuel,
Boosting mornings, oh so cool.
Life's bitter moments, stirred with cream,
A sweetened swirl of a crazy dream.

Caffeine laughs fill up the room,
As worries dissolve like sugar blooms.
With every drop, a story flows,
In the bottom of the cup, fun grows.

So raise your mugs to the brewed delight,
As darkness fades into morning light.
We sip through joy, we sip through woes,
A little laughter in every dose.

Reflections in a Coffeehouse.

From steaming mugs in cozy nooks,
We ponder life through coffee books.
With every chatter and whispered sigh,
We brew our thoughts like pumpkin pie.

The barista's tales, adorned with foam,
Turn strangers into friends, like coming home.
In every sip, a joke unfurls,
As milk dances like attractive swirls.

Chasing beans, we stumble and trip,
Every spill is a comic quip.
Laughter echoes from wall to wall,
Why spill the tea when coffee's our call?

So here's to cups that cheer us on,
With every brew, the day is dawn.
In steamy haze, we find our bliss,
Each sip an embrace, a frothy kiss.

Brewed Reflections

In porcelain cups, the world spins round,
With drips of joy that dance and sound.
Through coffee's eye, we see the fun,
As every pour draws in the sun.

Sipping slow, we find delight,
In awkward moments and quirky sights.
The espresso laugh, the latte sigh,
Each sip a wink, a playful high.

Friends gather close, sharing their brews,
With chocolate crumbs and silly news.
Laughter bubbles like water's roar,
A caffeinated chorus, who could ask for more?

So clink your cups, and raise a cheer,
To all the moments that bring good cheer.
In every drink, a story blends,
Grab a seat, where nonsense never ends.

Sips of Serenity

With every sip, my worries fade,
In a cozy nook, I'm unafraid.
Each flavor whispers, "Stay awhile,"
As mugs and smiles mix with style.

Coffee grounds, like secrets shared,
In frothy waves, I feel prepared.
A caramel drizzle dances sweet,
Like goofy tales on nimble feet.

So spill the beans and giggle loud,
In this coffee cloud, I'm so proud.
Life's brew is wild, but that's the charm,
A funny twist with every arm.

The last drop always tells a tale,
Of joyful sips and whimsical sail.
In mugs we trust, with hearts so light,
We sip and laugh into the night.

Surges of Solitude

In the quiet of the morning light,
Coffee brews, a glorious sight.
The world sleeps on, oblivious bliss,
While I sip my mug, a warm kiss.

Stirrings of thoughts, my mind's first brew,
Espresso dreams, oh, what to do?
Pajamas on, I take my stand,
A solo sip, my fate's unplanned.

Adventures await, I down the cup,
Just me, my brew, stirring things up.
Silent laughter fills the air,
With each gulp, I dare to care.

A solo act, a merry drink,
With every sip, I love to think.
In these moments, I'm never alone,
Just me and caffeine, in my zone.

Wake-Up Calls

The alarm rings loud, I hit the snooze,
But coffee whispers, 'You can't lose!'
A steaming mug, my morning fight,
With each brave gulp, I feel more bright.

Java jolts and mocha charms,
Awake, aware, with caffeine arms.
A ritual dance with frothy foam,
Transforming me to where I roam.

Pajama legs and bedhead flair,
Yet coffee's warmth, beyond compare.
A glorious brew, a sacred shindig,
Turns sleepy vibes to joyous gig.

Sipping slow, my spirit's call,
Through the steam, I rise, I fall.
In that cup, a world anew,
A daily shot, just me and brew.

Drips of Discovery

Pouring rain and coffee beans,
In every cup, hidden dreams.
With each drip, the truth unfolds,
In sips of wonder, brave and bold.

Bright light dances on the floor,
Curiosity knocks, I must explore.
I chase the steam like chasing a plan,
In java wisdom, I understand.

Coffee stains on a paper map,
With every sip, I close the gap.
Thoughts so wild, like caffeinated sprites,
In the warmth, I find my flights.

Frothy mysteries waiting to find,
With each sip, I free my mind.
So raise a cup to the great unknown,
In that dark brew, I've grown.

Sugar and Spice

A dash of sugar, a sprinkle of glee,
In my cup, what will I see?
Sprightly sips of sweet delight,
Turn the mundane to pure ignite.

Cinnamon whispers, nutmeg sings,
A festive dance of warm, sweet things.
Life's like coffee — bold, serene,
Twists and turns, the in-between.

A spoonful of cream, a twist of fate,
Each sip demands I contemplate.
With laughter brewed, in spice we trust,
Life's a blend, it's a must.

So let's fill our mugs, the day to please,
With sugar, spice, and easy breezes.
In this concoction, there's joy to find,
In every gulp, a friendly mind.

Beyond the Brew

Morning ritual, cup in hand,
A splash of chaos, grains of sand.
Caffeine dreams, a frothy flight,
Sipping sunshine, feeling bright.

Stirred and shaken, cream delight,
Sugar's dance, oh what a sight!
Watch me juggle, sip and spill,
Embrace the mess, it's all a thrill!

Mugs are clanking, laughter's loud,
Join the circus, coffee crowd.
Sip by sip, we share the fun,
In this brew, we find our sun.

Whipped Whispers

Froth like clouds, the cream will float,
Whispers sweet, on a coffee boat.
Take a gulp, and then a sigh,
A giggle tumbles as tastes fly.

Beans are chattering, tales unfold,
Mugs are filled, the warmth is bold.
Each sip tickles, a joyous tease,
With every pour, the heart finds ease.

Lattes laughing, marshmallows cheer,
Spoonful magic, hold it near.
In this cup, the humor swirls,
Happy dances, coffee girls!

The Essence of Espresso

Espresso shot, a tiny punch,
Wake-up calls, without a crunch.
In a thimble, bold and brash,
A jolt of joy, a caffeine splash.

Tiny cup of liquid glee,
Energized, come dance with me!
Double shot, it's quite a thrill,
Sipping quickly, what a skill!

Jokes abound in every brew,
Sips that spark, oh how they do!
With every gulp, the laughter grows,
In this brew, hilarity flows.

Stirred Stories

With a swirl, the story starts,
Coffee tales, we share our hearts.
Sugar mountains, cream cascades,
Sip by sip, the humor invades.

Stirred together, friends unite,
Laughter bubbles, mornings bright.
Every splash, a memory made,
In our mugs, no masquerade.

Steam rises, bringing cheer,
In this cup, we conquer fear.
Strained relations? Let's rewind!
Pour a brew, leave woes behind!

The Harvest of Hope

Beans in the sun, a curious sight,
Laughing at clouds that turn into night.
Pouring a brew, I watch it dance,
Each sip a giggle, a merry romance.

With frothy tops and creamy swirls,
Dreams bubble up like playful pearls.
A morning mug shines bright and bold,
Cheers to the stories that we are told.

Steam rising high, like wishes in air,
Caffeine's a trickster, it sparks with flair.
Every gulp whispers secrets of cheer,
Fueling my antics, let's toast with a beer!

The cup may spill, but don't shed a tear,
Just add some sugar, and laughter's near.
The harvest today yields smiles anew,
In every sip, I find something true.

Tasting Tomorrow

Wake up with coffee, the future looks bright,
Sipping and dreaming, what a delight!
A splash of milk, a dash of hope,
A frothy dream, oh how I cope!

Each drop a plan, each grind a goal,
Waking the dreams that stir in my soul.
Dancing with flavors, so wacky and bold,
I'm brewing adventures, let the stories unfold!

What's brewing today? A dash of despair,
But with each taste, it's lighter than air.
Stirring in laughter, a spoonful of glee,
Tomorrow's bright when you sip with me!

Pour some cream in and swirl it around,
Who knew the future could be so profound?
So clink your mugs, let's raise them high,
With each little sip, we'll soar in the sky.

Serendipity in Sips

Stumbling on coffee, a surprise in a mug,
Froth in my nose, oh, what a snug tug!
Sips of serendipity dance on my tongue,
Each gulp a rhythm, a song freshly sung.

Sugar and laughter, a perfect pair,
A jolt from the java, it's love in the air.
Downtrodden mornings turn upbeat and bright,
Thanks to my brew, I'm ready to fight!

The mug never judges, just warms up my hands,
Tales of the day are made in these strands.
With each funny spill, a new giggle grows,
Life's ups and downs taste sweet like a rose.

So let's brew a pot, bring the quirks out to play,
With serendipity steeping, come join the hooray!
In the land of the caffeinated, joy will abound,
For every sip savored, new wonders are found.

Journey in a Cup

I travel the globe with each little sip,
From beans in Brazil to Colombian quip.
A jolt from my mug takes me far and wide,
In the land of espresso, I'll take a ride!

Sipping on stories from people I meet,
Each cup an adventure, a little retreat.
I swirl the nuance, I savor the lore,
With every sweet sip, who knows what's in store?

The coffee grounds whisper of places unseen,
Bonding over brews like a fragrant cuisine.
From Turkish delights to lattes so sweet,
In each journey forward, oh, what a treat!

So pour me a cup, let's wander the breeze,
With coffee as compass, we'll do it with ease.
Together we'll laugh, together we'll roam,
For each coffee journey feels just like home.

Dark Roast Realities

In the morning grind, a ritual begins,
Coffee stains on my shirt like life's little sins.
Strong brew ignites the sleepy little brain,
But somehow I still forget where I've lain.

Sips of black gold chase the snooze away,
Each gulp a promise to make it through the day.
I spill dreams in my cup every dawn, you see,
Each drop's a tiny joke, laughing back at me.

Beans of Belonging

Gathered 'round a table with laughter and cheer,
A pot brews stories, our worries disappear.
Beans from afar, with tales yet untold,
In this warm coffee house, we're rich, not just bold.

A dash of sugar and a sprinkle of spice,
In every warm sip, oh, the friendships are nice.
We share silly secrets while sipping our brew,
With each little laugh, our hearts blend like two.

Steeped in Moments

Watch the kettle whistle, a comedic affair,
I trip on the rug, who put it there?
The tea bags giggle while the coffee beans sigh,
Each steeped moment's a reason to fly.

Pouring in chaos like a dance in a storm,
Mugs clink together, it feels so warm.
Every drop's a chapter in this brew-tiful tale,
Smiles all around, it's a laugh-filled gale.

The Language of Lattes

Foamy hearts and swirls, art on my mug,
Translating my feelings; it's a warm, cozy hug.
Skipped my morning jog, but no need for regret,
Caffeine's my buddy; we're a perfect duet.

With whipped cream mountains and sprinkles on top,
I ponder my dreams while I slurp and I stop.
Every sip is a giggle, a frothy delight,
In this caffeinated circus, I'll toast to the night.

The Daily Grind

Each morning starts with a splat,
Coffee on my favorite hat.
The pot's whistle sings so clear,
A ritual I hold so dear.

Espresso shots and frothy peaks,
I spill my thoughts, then laugh at tweaks.
The mug hugs my hands with cheer,
Fueling my day, oh so sincere.

Stirs of joy, a splash of cream,
In every sip, a waking dream.
Toast to the beans that know my name,
In this caffeinated game of fame.

Caffeine Chronicles

Once upon a morning bright,
I brewed a storm with all my might.
The coffee danced, it swirled and spun,
In every drop, a tale begun.

Java jests and mocha dreams,
Froth and steam complete the schemes.
Each sip a twist, a plot unfold,
In caffeine's grip, the brave and bold.

Yet through each sip, a lesson learned,\nFor every cup, a grind's returned.
Life's beans, though bitter, sweetly blend,
Cheers to the brew that's a trusty friend.

A Cup Full of Dreams

In a porcelain vessel, hopes reside,
A splash of daydreams, worlds collide.
Swirls of sugar, nothing to lose,
With every gulp, my future enthuse.

Stirring visions, frothy delight,
What's right becomes whimsically slight.
Espresso shots keep the laughs alive,
In a cup full of dreams, I thrive.

Coffee spills like candid tales,
Through highs and lows, it never fails.
With every taste, absurd and bright,
Life's mysteries brew on this delight.

Bitter and Sweet

A blend of dark with sprinkles bright,
Brewed wisdom wakes me with delight.
Each sip unpacks the tangled mess,
Sweet thoughts emerge, a funny dress.

Some days it's bitter, some days it's sweet,
With every cup, I dance on my feet.
Beans of chaos, joy on repeat,
In this caffeinated, lively feat.

Laughter bubbles, like foam on top,
Even when things seem to flop.
In mugs we hold, we sip and sigh,
A blend of moments that fly high.

Caffeine Chronicles

Morning brew, a jolt to start,
Like a tiny rocket for the heart.
Sipping slowly, with a grin,
Wondering where my thoughts have been.

Espresso shots, a daring feat,
Like a dance party for my feet.
Laughter bubbles, steam arises,
In this cup, no room for sizes.

Each drip tells tales from afar,
Of sleepy heads and coffee bars.
Stirred with joy, like cream in brew,
A caffeinated point of view.

So grab a cup, and share a cheer,
With every sip, let laughter steer.
In this blend, we find our way,
As coffee makes us laugh all day.

Frothy Epiphanies

In the morning, pot is brewing,
Coffee beans are gently stewing.
A frothy crown atop each mug,
Wish I could give a coffee hug.

Walking in, it smells like cheer,
This cozy cup is always near.
It whispers secrets, warm and bold,
In every sip, a tale unfolds.

From cappuccino's fluffy foam,
To dark roast's robust little home.
Each flavor blends a funny scene,
Of sleepy heads and caffeine dreams.

Pour another, let's have fun,
In this café, we've just begun.
With each slurp and spirited cheer,
We toast to moments, bright and clear.

Beanstalk of Being

Pour it strong, pour it bold,
Magic in the cup, behold!
With every sip, I climb so high,
To java lands beyond the sky.

The aroma lifts, a merry song,
In this wilderness, I belong.
Frothy clouds and laughter blend,
A bean-filled journey with no end.

Oh, coffee king, oh, queen of cream,
Your essence fuels my wildest dream.
With each gulp, I chuckle loud,
Who knew a bean could be so proud?

So hold your cup and raise it high,
Let's sip together, you and I.
In the beanstalk of this brew,
We find a world that's bright and new.

The Mug of Memories

In the morning, make no fuss,
Grab the mug, share a plus.
Each slurp recalls a funny tale,
Of coffee spills and wild email.

With friends around, the cup we sip,
Every laugh, a joyful trip.
Creamy swirls like memories flow,
Warm reminders of laughter's glow.

From café corners to kitchen stalls,
This trusty mug knows it all.
Each gulp's a snapshot in our book,
Just take a sip, and take a look.

So here's to moments, rich and blend,
With coffee laughter, time won't end.
Holding stories in a cup so bright,
The mug of memories, pure delight.

Steam and Shadows

In the morning, a cup starts to brew,
Poured with care, a ritual so true.
Steam rises up like dreams in the air,
Swirls of aroma, a love affair.

Pour it too fast, and it might spill,
Just like my plans, slipping down the hill.
I sip and I laugh at my daily grind,
With coffee in hand, I pretend to unwind.

A dash of cream for a touch of flair,
Sweet like my jokes, if anyone dares.
Espresso shots giving courage to try,
To tackle the day, oh my, oh me, oh my!

Each mug tells a tale, all brewed to delight,
With smiles and puns, we share every bite.
So here's to the steam that fills up our space,
And shadows of laughter, oh what a place!

The Final Sip

The clock ticks softly, as I take my stand,
Just one more cup, it's somehow all planned.
With every gulp, I'm one step ahead,
But too much caffeine, and I'll end up in bed!

I glance at the dregs, so dark and profound,
The bottom of life, where lost dreams are found.
It's a bittersweet dance, I take every drop,
Each sip's a comedian, I wish it would stop!

Can it be magic or just plain old beans?
It fuels my adventure and sparks all my dreams.
A dash of the absurd keeps me on my toes,
Like waking from naps that I never chose.

The laughter that bubbles with every last sip,
While visions of sugar plums don't quite equip.
So I toast to the mug, that's my faithful mate,
For the joy in the journey, never too late!

Caffeine and Contemplation

In a café corner, all cozy and bright,
I ponder my existence, oh what a sight!
With a latte in hand, I take a deep breath,
Counting my blessings instead of my debts.

My thoughts swirl around like milk in the cup,
What's my next move? When will I wise up?
Should I live like my coffee? Strong, bold, and hot?
Or soft like the foam, all frothy and caught?

A scone on the side offers sweet company,
And crumbs on the table match thoughts of me.
The barista winks, a curious delight,
While I scheme my escape from this caffeine-filled night.

Each gulp's a new venture, brewed fresh from the past,
Mixing laughter and ponder, making moments last.
So here's to the café, our thoughts intertwined,
With caffeine-fueled wisdom, oh look what we find!

Morning's Warm Embrace

Waking up grouchy, what's that in my cup?
A piping hot brew, it's draped like a hug.
Coffee's warm whisper says, 'Hey, rise and shine!'
With each gentle sip, I feel divine!

The sun peeks in, with a wink and a grin,
As I toast my mug, cheers to all things akin!
Forgotten are worries, the trials from last night,
At the dawn of each day, my spark feels so bright!

A sprinkle of laughter, the flavor of cheer,
A hint of adventure, for breakfast I steer.
This warm amaretto lifts my spirits high,
Like laughter from friends who just drop by.

So here's to the mornings, where joy takes its place,
To the warmth in my cup and the smiles on each face.
With every last drop, I'm ready to sway,
In the dance of the dawn, come what may!

Fragments of Flavor

Beans dance in the grinder's whir,
A symphony of scents, a caffeinated purr.
Laughter bubbles in the frothy cup,
As caffeine kicks in, we perk right up.

Sips of joy, with each cheerful taste,
No moment wasted, never a haste.
Sugar sprinkles like confetti bright,
In this merry brew, everything's right.

Espresso shots like dreams that soar,
One more cup, then maybe four!
Stirring in chaos, a splash of cream,
We caffeinate our way through the steam.

So here's to the mugs that overflow,
With giggles and grinds, what a show!
Each drop a joke, a moment's cheer,
Who knew hot beans could bring such jeer?

Ristretto Revelations

A little shot, a little fun,
Ristretto laughter, brews begun.
Strong and bold, like a dad joke told,
Each cup reveals secrets so bold.

Stirring in sugar, a wink and grin,
Life's quirks bubble up from within.
It's all in the froth, a tickle or two,
Coffee tales shared, both silly and true.

We stumble through mornings, caffeine in hand,
Mugs like trophies, together we stand.
With each warm sip, a giggle escapes,
As we sip and slurp from our funny shapes.

Let's toast to dark brews and light-hearted puns,
To frothy adventures, and caffeine runs.
For in every cup lies a moment to share,
With friends and with laughter, we float on air.

A Symphony in Steam

Whirls of steam rise like joyous tunes,
Steam whistles softly, morning's maroons.
A dance of aromas, a tangled brew,
Mirth in a mug, funny tales anew.

Coffee grounds scatter like confetti bright,
A party of flavors, a hilarious sight.
Pouring patience while the kettle sings,
Each brew like magic, with laughter it brings.

With each sip, quirky joy fills the air,
Who knew dark beans could spread such flair?
A splash of wit, a twist of fate,
We wrap our mornings in warmth, and relate.

So celebrate each drip and grumble,
In this coffee chaos, there's no need to stumble.
For happiness brews in cups, it's clear,
And every laugh is like a foamy cheer!

Tasting the Today

Awake to sunshine, the kettle's call,
Mug in hand, we conquer it all.
Pour the magic, watch it swirl,
In this coffee world, we giggle and twirl.

Flavors collide, a circus of beans,
Each sip brings smiles, or so it seems.
Spilling coffee like my thoughts today,
Oops! That's just part of the funny ballet.

Dripping dreams in a cerulean cup,
Stirring up grins, we just can't stop.
Living in moments, one sip at a time,
Finding the humor, like sweet coffee rhyme.

So here's to the brews and goofy delight,
To quirky mornings and friends holding tight.
With every laugh and froth we enjoy,
Today's a cup full of fun, oh boy!

Out of the Pot

Morning's brew, a bubbling cheer,
Pour it strong, let worries disappear.
Caffeine jitters, a dance so spry,
With every sip, I dream to fly.

Caramel whispers, a sweet embrace,
Espresso shots, a quick-paced race.
Misplaced spoons, the search is on,
Did I take my cup, or was it gone?

Creamy clouds rise, a frothy tide,
Chasing lattes, we take the ride.
Oh, the stories that mugs can tell,
In cozy cafes, we sip so well.

Together we laugh, the world's a joke,
With every cappuccino, we provoke.
So gear up, friends, the pot won't wait,
Pour your joy, and celebrate fate!

The Depth of Drip

Sitting quiet, the drips come slow,
A rhythm that starts with a morning glow.
Measuring grounds, a precise art,
Like life's moments, we play our part.

Drip, drip, drop, the clock ticks on,
Wondering where all my tips have gone.
Coffee spills, a paint of brown,
Covering chaos in this small town.

Brewing troubles, let them steep,
A warm cup makes the world less deep.
Pouring some thoughts, let's chat away,
Stirring up dreams, come what may.

With every cup, our stories blend,
Laughs and sighs, we never end.
So here's a toast, to drip and drop,
Embrace the brew, we'll never stop!

Cafe Encounters

In the queue, a friendly glance,
Baristas dance, a caffeinated trance.
With every order, a new delight,
Espresso whispers in the soft light.

Paper cups clink, ideas fly,
Over iced drinks, we reach for the sky.
French press chats, the time lapses,
Laughing hard over cappuccino mishaps.

Sugar spills, a sticky mess,
Muffins shared help ease the stress.
With new friends, we dive right in,
Add a splash of chaos to the din.

Oh, the tales that brew in this space,
From sips of joy to joy's embrace.
So grab your cup, keep it near,
Life's a cafe, let's spread the cheer!

Aromatic Adventures

Waking up to a scent divine,
Bean dreams floating, all is fine.
Roasting tales in the morning sun,
Adventure awaits, so let's have fun.

Frothy mountains, a whipped delight,
Stir it up, let flavors ignite.
Diving deep into the cup's abyss,
Each sip a treasure, can't resist.

Herbal wonders, a calming spell,
In every pour, there's magic to tell.
Trim the chaos, enjoy the blend,
With each adventure, new plots extend.

So raise your mug, let's seize the day,
With laughter rich, we'll find our way.
To the grind and brew, we stake our claim,
In this aromatic, joyous game!

Roasted Realities

In the cup, a darkened swirl,
Dreams brewed with a little twirl.
Every sip, a bizarre plot,
What's wished might just be a lot.

The beans say, "Just take a chance!"
Yet every cup seems to dance.
A splash of cream, a dash of thrill,
Reality? It gives me chills.

Sometimes it's bitter, sometimes sweet,
With a sprinkle of sugar, can't be beat.
But don't expect it to stay hot,
Like life and coffee, it's all a plot.

So raise your mug to dreams amiss,
Each sip's a chance, a slurp of bliss.
When in doubt, just brew away,
Tomorrow's beans will surely play.

Creamed Aspirations

A frothy latte, dreams all frosted,
Ambitions rise, but not to be lost-ed.
A dash of syrup, a sprinkle of hope,
But oh dear, let's not elope!

Whipped cream mountains, goals in sight,
Yet some days it's just a fight.
Too many flavors cloud the way,
Guess it's a mocha kinda day!

Stir the pot, but watch the spills,
Too much fun can give me chills.
Yet, every sip tastes like a jest,
Oh, sweet cream, you know me best.

So here's to hopes, both bright and bold,
With coffee dreams that never get old.
Through steam and froth, we'll find our way,
In every sip, we laugh and play.

Dregs of the Day

The mug is empty, thoughts dismay,
Is that the end of joyous play?
Remnants linger, coffee's ghost,
Did I even brew? I cringe, it's the most.

Leftover grounds, they tell their tale,
Cling to the cup like a ship to sail.
But each dark swallow, bitter and bold,
Wraps up the day like stories told.

A flick of foam, a splash of fate,
Life's late-night brew always tempts debate.
With every gulp, the wisdom flows,
Even dregs hold secrets, this much I know.

Tomorrow's beans will wake me bright,
To chase the joy, to find the light.
For now, I leave the dregs behind,
In coffee's charm, I'm not confined.

Sip by Sip

A steaming cup, a moment's clench,
Take it slow, don't ever wrench.
Sip by sip, the joy unfolds,
A daily thrill that never gets old.

Laughter bubbles like a brew,
Each drop's a joke, a funny view.
Stir the chaos, watch it spin,
What humor drips from deep within?

Froth on top, some laughter too,
A pinch of love in every hue.
So coffee, dear, let's share a grin,
With every sip, it's where we begin.

In the warm embrace of fragrant nights,
Let's laugh until the morning lights.
Raise your mugs to whims and fun,
For with a sip, the day's just begun.

The Aroma of Existence

In the morning, coffee brews,
Awakening sleepy blues.
A dash of cream, a sprinkle of luck,
Sip too fast, and you might get stuck.

Espresso shots and laughter shared,
Groggy friends who never cared.
Stirring dreams in a ceramic cup,
Watch the world wake, then lift it up.

Frothy clouds dance in the sky,
With every sip, the worries fly.
Caffeine giggles, in zany spirals,
Chasing the day like playful trials.

Life's a latte, thick and sweet,
With every gulp, new tastes to meet.
So take a sip, let worries go,
Pour a little joy, let good times flow.

Mugs and Memories

Gather 'round, the mugs collide,
Filling hearts with liquid pride.
Candles lit, we sip and chat,
Stains of humor in the mat.

Rough days steep like a strong brew,
The laughter flows; we spill the hue.
Mugs in hand, tales come alive,
Coffee-fueled, we start to thrive.

Each sip a snapshot, warmth inside,
In the swirl of steam, we slide.
Brewed connections, rich and deep,
Memories linger, never sleep.

From empty cups, new hopes arise,
As laughter rises, truth belies.
Every memory brewed in sync,
In bitter sweet, we pause and think.

Steaming Journeys

On a road trip with coffee in hand,
Navigating life's wonderland.
A travel mug, a map unrolled,
Adventures shared, a story told.

Frothy drinks and snack-filled bags,
Rolling laughter, gypsy gags.
Detours taken, coffee breaks,
In the chaos, joy awakes.

Bumpy roads and coffee stains,
Hypothesize while it rains.
Toasting cups at every stop,
In steaming cups, the world won't drop.

The journey steams, much like the brew,
Turn the page for something new.
So fill your cup, let worries flee,
In every sip, find jubilee.

Grounds for Thought

Sipping slowly on a thought,
In the dregs, wisdom's caught.
The grounds awaken, tales to tell,
In every sip, a jesting spell.

Stirring up both truth and fun,
Swirling fables, everyone.
A coffee cup, a thoughtful pause,
Questions linger; we have our cause.

Fleeting moments, friends explode,
In caffeine-fueled episodes.
Laugh lines deepen, cups unite,
As we ponder with delight.

So grab your cup and take a chance,
In every pour, a goofy dance.
Grounds for thought amidst the cheer,
With every sip, let's hold it dear.

Liquid Motivation

In the morning, I stumble, oh dear,
My coffee's the answer, it's clear.
A splash of caffeine, a touch of delight,
Turns my grumpiness into a flight.

With every sip, I feel inspired,
Energized thoughts that I've acquired.
But if it's decaf, don't be surprised,
Just me and my nap, unceremoniously compromised.

My cup's like my buddy, always near,
With smiles and warmth, it brings cheer.
Pour it black, or add some cream,
In the coffee realm, I'm the queen of the dream!

So raise your mug; let's toast away,
To every laugh we have today.
For in this brew, we find our starts,
Liquid motivation fills our hearts.

The Coffeehouse Diaries

In a café bustling with cheer,
I take my seat, the end is near.
With lattes dancing and scones galore,
I soak in the chaos, then I explore.

The barista winks, mischief in hand,
"I hear your dreams! Can I make them grand?"
I order a mocha with a fancy name,
Just hoping the taste isn't all just a game.

A couple near me, deep in a talk,
While I sip my drink, they giggle and squawk.
Their problems seem tiny; love's a froth,
While I'm just here for a caffeine broth.

As people pass with their trendy cups,
I wonder how many went for the pup cups.
In the coffeehouse, we spill our beans,
A confessional space for life's quirky scenes.

Warmth in a Cup

Steam rises high, in late morning sun,
Holding this mug, my day's just begun.
Chocolate swirls and a dash of spice,
Every sip taken, oh so nice!

I guard this warmth like a prized gem,
My comfy sweater, my little hymn.
With a muffin on the side, crumbly and sweet,
Is there a better way to greet?

I spill some on the table, oops, what a mess!
But the laughter that follows? Pure happiness!
The maid grudgingly wipes with hardly a smile,
While I sip my drink and stay for a while.

This mug is my shield, from troubles afar,
In the world of coffee, I'm a superstar.
So lift your cups to the warmth we share,
And let the buzz worry away our cares!

Simple Pleasures

Pouring my coffee, feeling so grand,
With the perfect amount, just as I planned.
Adding sugar, a swirl here and there,
These little moments, they leave us bare.

A cozy corner in my favorite spot,
A novel in hand, giving my thoughts a shot.
With every sip, I pause and reflect,
On simple pleasures one must not neglect.

The aroma floating, dances in air,
I daydream of travels, places to share.
A café in Paris, or beaches in Spain,
But for now, this cup, my joy, my gain.

So cheers to the brews that fill our days,
In their warm embraces, our worries ablaze.
In every drip, there's a story untold,
Simple pleasures, worth more than gold.

Flavorful Epiphanies

One sip in, the world is bright,
Thoughts take flight, whatever's right.
With every swirl, ideas brew,
As froth cascades, dreams come true.

Stir in a smile, sugar and cream,
A dash of chaos, or so it seems.
Espresso shots like truth bombs hit,
Gulp it down, embrace the wit.

A coffee cup holds wisdom vast,
More lessons learned from sips amassed.
It percolates through joy and strife,
A frothy mix of silly life.

So let's toast to every blend,
The quirks that brew, the laughs we spend.
In every cup, a tale we find,
The merry grind of the everyday mind.

Not Just Caffeine

Pour it strong, and pour it bold,
Conversations start, stories told.
With every drip, a chuckle flows,
The laughs erupt where caffeine goes.

Play with flavors, don't be shy,
Pumpkin spice or mocha high?
A concoction sparked, ideas ignite,
Sip up the humor, feel the light.

Baristas know our quirks by heart,
A latte swirl, a frothy art.
No secrets stay in coffee's grip,
It's like a party in every sip.

So when you're down, or feeling blue,
Remember beans can comfort too.
In every cup, find joy anew,
A brew's the friend that understands you.

Brews and Blues

When morning dawns, dreams go astray,
But coffee's there to save the day.
A splash of joy in liquid form,
A quirky dance, a cozy warm.

Drip, drip, drip, the routine's here,
But add some laughter, bring the cheer.
Mugs clink together, stories shared,
When coffee's in hand, no one's scared.

Froth on top like clouds of fun,
Sip it slow, don't rush the run.
With every gulp, a twist, a grin,
In every cup, the joy begins.

So grab a seat and take a break,
With every pour, the laughter wakes.
In steamy cups, the blues dissolve,
In coffee's warmth, we find resolve.

The Comfort of Concoctions

Hot or cold, it warms the soul,
Each unique brew, a savory bowl.
From bitter notes to sweet surprises,
Caffeine fixes all our crises.

In quirky mugs, our stories spin,
The wisdom shared, where to begin?
With cream and sugar, chaos reigns,
Coffee's joy covers all our pains.

Sips of comfort in every blend,
Finding solace, a trusty friend.
Let's raise a cup to all we face,
In funny brews, we find our place.

So bring the beans and laughter loud,
In every cup, we're feeling proud.
With a jolt of joy and a grin so wide,
Let's celebrate the brew by our side.

Batching Bravery

Each morning starts with a cup so bold,
A ritual of warmth, a story untold.
With splashes of cream, I craft my flair,
Turns out I'm a barista unaware.

The kettle sings tunes of courage and cheer,
While I battle my fears with caffeine near.
I sip on my dreams, in mugs like a shield,
In this java kingdom, I refuse to yield.

At work, I'm a warrior, fueled by the brew,
Dodging deadlines like they're frothy fondue.
With espresso shots piercing through my haze,
I conquer the chaos in its milky praise.

With each bitter sip, I chuckle and grin,
A fool with a smile, where folly begins.
So here's to my courage, served steaming and hot,
In the café of bravado, I take my shot.

Percolated Profoundness

In the grounds of existence, I ponder and stir,
Espressos of wisdom that shimmer and blur.
As I watch the drip dance down to the pot,
I laugh at the things that I've learned and forgot.

The filter of life holds the grinds of my fears,
As I brew all my thoughts through the laughter and tears.
With each little splash, a thought ricochets,
Coffee grounds whisper, 'Just open your gaze.'

A scoop of this flavor, a dash of that hue,
The palette of mornings, forever anew.
I lift up my cup, a beacon, a guide,
For in sips of compassion, our truths reside.

So here's to the moments of richness and glee,
While swirling our worries in caffeinated spree.
These sips full of magic, both bitter and bright,
Will brew up our futures with joy in each bite.

Fragrant Futures

The aroma of dawn beckons me near,
With dreams in the steam, and a grin from ear to ear.
I brew up my hopes in a cup of delight,
Each sip is a promise that shines oh so bright.

As the froth floats above, ideas take flight,
With flavors that dance in the morning light.
With sugar and spice, my visions unfold,
Fragrant futures simmer, both silly and bold.

My mug's overflowing with possibilities,
Mixing zany thoughts with a dash of old teas.
With laughter as latte and whimsy on pour,
I'll hop on this caffeine cloud, ready to soar!

So cheers to the brews that ignite our desire,
For even the wildest dreams might catch fire.
With cups at the ready, let's savor the quest,
In the café of futures, we'll find our zest.

Cups of Connection

Gather round, friends, with your mugs nice and warm,
In coffee's embrace, we weather the storm.
With laughter and latte art shared in delight,
Our spirits unite, like sugar and spice.

Each sip is a toast to the bonds that we share,
Over coffee concoctions, we shed every care.
Espresso-filled moments, we hold them so dear,
In this caffeinated circle, there's nothing to fear.

The clink of the mugs rings like bells in the air,
With stories and smiles, our joy we declare.
From cappuccino capers to mental retreats,
We brew up connections, oh isn't it sweet?

So raise up your cup, let's honor this brew,
For every warm sip brings me closer to you.
In flavors of friendship, our hearts intertwine,
With cups full of laughter, let's savor the climb.

www.ingramcontent.com/pod-product-compliance
Lightning Source LLC
Chambersburg PA
CBHW051650160426
43209CB00004B/856